AF488027

It's Already Alright

An Ode to the Losers

REGGEE BONEY

© 2026 by Reggee Boney

All rights reserved.

No part of this publication may be reproduced, distributed, or transmitted in any form or by any means, including photocopying, recording, or other electronic or mechanical methods, without the prior written permission of the publisher.

Published by Designed for Greatness, LLC

Atlanta, Georgia

ISBN: 979-8-9918242-9-3

First Edition

Printed in the United States of America

Dedication

To all the losers who keep showing up.

Author's Note

There are some things you write because you've won. This is not one of them. This is a book I wrote because I have lost...a lot.

If you are holding this book along with the weight of failure, know that this book is not a five-step plan or formula. It is a hand on your shoulder, a hug, a holy reminder for the days you don't have eloquent words to pray; a reminder that between then, now, and what is to come, it's already alright.

-reggee boney

About the Author

Reggee Boney is a legally-trained ordained minister who knows what it means to live with failure and keep showing up. Drawing from years of experience in advocacy, ministry, and personal goals and setbacks, he writes simply in this work to remind all the "losers" that their loss is not the end of their story. Originally from Durham, North Carolina, Reggee resides in the Chicago suburb of Oak Park, Illinois with his wife and three children.

A graduate of North Carolina Central University, Duke University Divinity School, and the University of North Carolina at Chapel Hill School of Law, Reggee's writings blend the law, theology, and lived experiences to speak extraordinary hope into unfinished lives.

Start
Finish

When it seems like the beginning will
also be your ending remember...

it's already alright.

EVERYONE
ELSE

When everyone else seems to win,
but your victories are looking thin
remember...

it's already alright.

When the sun shines on them, but your
cloud rains with grim remember...

it's already alright.

When you fail and fail again, with no strength to try within remember...

it's already alright.

When darkness is day and night seem
to stay remember...

it's already alright.

RIP
HOPES &
DREAMS

When the dream is deferred, and your
hope is interred remember...

it's already alright.

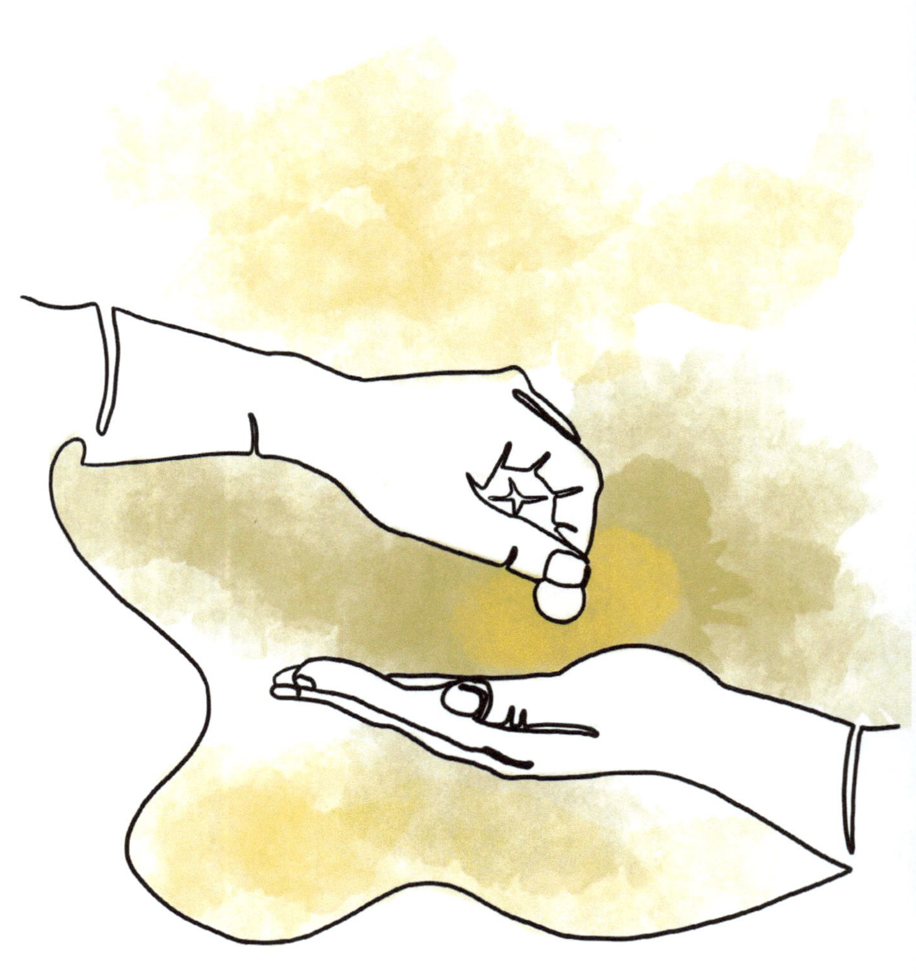

When your money is funny and your
change is strange remember...

it's already alright.

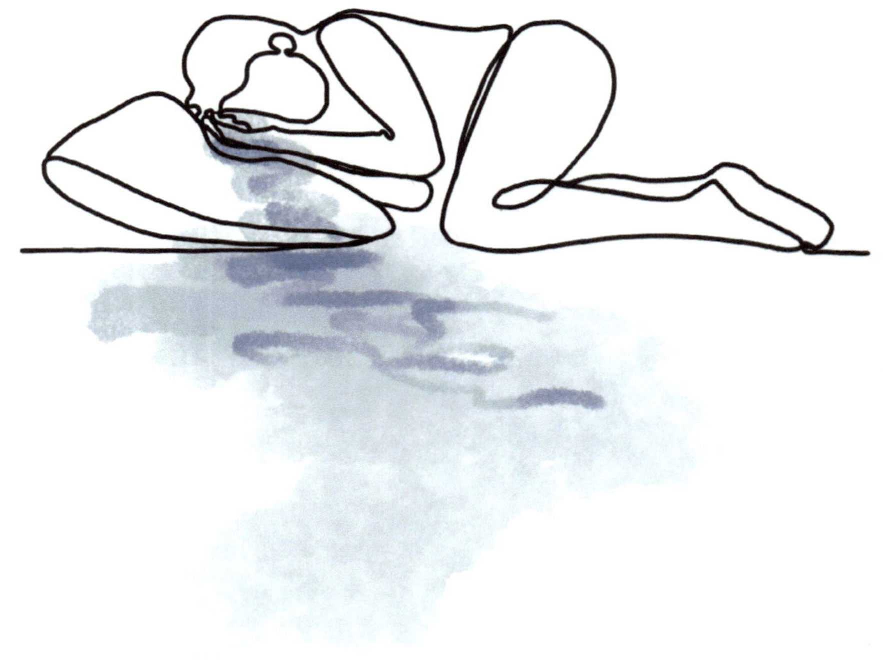

When your pillow is wet with tears
from all of your doubts and fears
remember...

it's already alright.

When friends are few and family is
through remember...

it's already alright.

Because time will bring both good and
bad things

As life will give even as it takes

The sun will shine, the rain will fall, the
wind will blow, you'll stand you'll fall

You'll grieve, you'll cry, you'll laugh
and sigh

But when—not *if*—you lose and get stuck

in the mire and life's muck...

Good Things
Beginning
Bad Things
Ending

Just know bad things must come to an
end

As good things come to those that
contend

But GREAT things come to those who
fight

Who show up, even when nothing
seems right

Because sometimes showing up *is* the win

So, when they don't clap, show up again

To let them know despite the night,

the earth will keep spinning and bring
sunlight

And in the morning, when you're still
here

You'll prove that bad days only make it
clear

That new beginnings come after night

So, remember...

it's already alright.

www.ingramcontent.com/pod-product-compliance
Lightning Source LLC
Chambersburg PA
CBHW040917110726
48005CB00006B/925